BRICKS *Without Straw*

How Homeschooling Can Make Your Role as a Christian Parent Easier

Trina Kay Lewis

WestBow Press books may be ordered through booksellers or by contacting:

WestBow Press
A Division of Thomas Nelson & Zondervan
1663 Liberty Drive
Bloomington, IN 47403
www.westbowpress.com
1 (866) 928-1240

ISBN: 978-1-5127-8164-9 (sc)
ISBN: 978-1-5127-8163-2 (e)

Library of Congress Control Number: 2017904921

Print information available on the last page.

WestBow Press rev. date: 4/12/2017

Acknowledgements

I would like to express my sincere gratitude to several special people in my life.

To my husband, John, confident and tender, thank you for your unending love. You are my best friend and excellent leader; there is no one I would rather be with than you. It will be an honor to grow old with you.

And my children – you are a great joy in my life.

Brett, strong and intelligent, yet generous and kind, thank you for allowing me opportunities to share my heart with you. I treasure our relationship and am very proud of you.

To Megan, Brett's wife and my friend, noble and steadfast, thank you for loving my son and being his incredible helper. Thank you also for caring for the young people in our community.

Kim, thank you for being exactly who you are – courageous and capable, gracious and merciful. You are loved, respected, valued and admired by so many and I deeply value our friendship.

James, wise beyond your years, thank you for caring so deeply. Your selfless nature and passionate dedication to the Savior merits emulation. I am excited to see how the Lord will use your life for His kingdom.

And

Melanie, talented and gentle, thank you for your careful, thoughtful ways. You are a lovely young woman, graceful and compassionate; a precious gem. I treasure your friendship.

To my parents.

Bill, my dad, faithful and esteemed, thank you for always believing in me. When I told you I was going to write this book, you encouraged me by saying that I should because I was an expert. You have always been like that towards me and I am grateful that you are my Dad.

To Sheila, my mom, generous, energetic, and beautiful, you are cherished and adored by THE Father. Thank you for being my mommy. I realize now that I want to be just like you.

Thank you, Dad and Mom, for loving me even through the sins of my youth.

To Jeff, my brother, loyal and trustworthy, my very first playmate and companion, thank you for still being my friend. Your care for your family is remarkable and you are clearly adored.

Thank you all for your sweet contributions to my life. You are dearly loved.

Contents

Introduction ix

My Story xi

Chapter 1—The Essentials 1

Chapter 2—The Home in Homeschooling 11

Chapter 3—The School in Homeschooling 17

Chapter 4—Choosing Curricula 28

Chapter 5—Life in the Middle of Your School 40

Chapter 6—It's Not Just About the Books 53

Bibliography Notes 63

Introduction

> As for man, his days are like grass; he flourishes like a flower of the field; for the wind passes over it, and it is gone, and its place knows it no more. But the steadfast love of the Lord is from everlasting to everlasting on those who fear him, and his righteousness to children's children, to those who keep his covenant and remember to do his commandments. The Lord has established his throne in the heavens, and his kingdom rules over all.
>
> —Psalm 103:15-19 ESV

The house is rather quiet these days. Our children are living their own lives now. Our decisions for them have been made and those decisions have been lived out. The time for second guessing is over. While there are many things I wish I had known then or had done differently, as I stand here on the other side of our homeschooling adventure, I can declare with complete honesty that there is one thing I know for sure: I am so glad we schooled our children at home. In that decision I have no regrets.

Did we make all of the right choices? Of course not! There were certainly missteps along the way. Like the time I mistakenly gave my daughter a quiz out of her brother's math book and then fussed at her when she told me that she did not understand the concepts. Or the time I insisted on having summer school and made everyone miserable until July. Or the time … well you get my point.

As Courtney Reissig reflects in her book "The Accidental Feminist",

> I am not the model. But the model was never meant to be you or me anyway. I've got a newsflash for you: perfection is not attainable. Perfection was only attained by one person, Christ.[1]

Like many, I often learn from my mistakes. Please join me, a retired veteran of the homeschooling trenches, as I share some of the things I learned from those mistakes, some things that worked well for us and some practical advice. Allow me, through this book, to hopefully give you a vision for your homeschooling journey and the encouragement to carry on.

It is worth it.

My Story

> There is no fear in love, but perfect love casts out fear.
>
> —1 John 4:18a ESV

I remember when I first heard about schooling options. I had never really thought about it before. I just assumed that children go to school. Once someone asked me if I had gone to public school and, frankly, I didn't even know what she was talking about. Did she mean the school down the street from our house? The one where the school bus took me every day? Was that a public school? Was that not just "school"? Were there choices?

Well, yes, apparently, there were choices, and discussions of these options were dominating playdate conversations among the young moms in my church. I was beginning to feel subtly pressured to make a good choice. I certainly didn't want to mindlessly move forward with public school, but private school seemed like a financial burden and I knew practically nothing about homeschooling. Although I dearly loved my children and cherished our time together, it made me nervous to consider being with them all day, every day. I utilized naptime to accomplish tasks that proved difficult to manage with young ones underfoot. How would it possibly work to have boisterous school-aged children around all day? How much stress would I be under if their education depended solely on me? These questions seemed to add a huge burden to my already overworked status.

One morning I was pushing my side-by-side double stroller through the narrow church hallway, having difficulty maneuvering its wide base, when an acquaintance approached us. She asked if the older children were going to start school in the fall. My five-year-old twins were each holding onto a side of the stroller and my infant twins (yes, you read that correctly) were each strapped into a seat. My Bible, notebook, and diaper bag were stuffed into the back of the stroller and my purse hung precariously on my shoulder. I replied "yes" and she asked if I had thought about homeschooling.

Although she was probably a very sweet lady, when I revisit that day in my mind, I am tempted to recall her as a tall, intimidating woman carrying a clipboard and wearing glasses that slid down her nose so she had to look over them to see me. In my imagination, she had a pencil placed behind her ear and looked as if she was ready to record my answer and give it directly to Jesus. I do not remember exactly how I answered her, but I do remember feeling so overwhelmed by the thought of adding something (and particularly something that big) to my plate that I wanted to cry.

I tucked away that brief conversation along with the ones I was overhearing from the other moms and we continued to live life. The older twins, Brett and Kim, went to public school that fall and I concentrated on caring for our two babies, James and Melanie, my husband, and our home. I also volunteered in the local school once a week.

But soon I began to feel God gently tugging at my heart about homeschooling. I kept stumbling onto articles on the subject, meeting ladies who were doing it well, hearing success stories, and even being invited to seminars. And, although the two oldest were in an excellent magnet program in what was considered the number one ranking school system in the country, Fairfax County Virginia in the suburbs of our nation's capital, I just didn't have a peace about it. It appeared to be academically exemplary, but it just didn't feel quite right when I dropped them off each morning.

To add to my confusion things were not going well for me personally. My husband was not yet a believer and we had difficulties in our marriage. So, I hesitated and stumbled around a bit. By this time Brett and Kim were in second grade and James and Melanie were toddlers.

Having only been a Christian for a few years at this point, perhaps I was not yet familiar with hearing God's voice or perhaps I was afraid to obey (or maybe a little of both), so I dug my feet in. Certainly, in my circumstance, sending my children to public school was the right thing, I thought often. But God continued to make it evident that He didn't want my children there. Finally, I went to John and asked if he thought we should consider homeschooling. His answer was brief and final -- "No, that's weird", he said, firmly. So, having obeyed God, I laid it down.

I grin as I write this because (obviously) John came to feel differently and has become one of the biggest advocates of homeschooling that I know. Also, in God's beautiful and merciful plan, he saved my dear husband and our lives were forever changed.

Not long after our "conversation", one of John's friends, who was a homeschooling dad, told him about the benefits of their school choice. John's interest was piqued. When he got to know this man's children, who were polite and able to interact intelligently with adults, his mind was changed and he told me I could school the kids at home if I wanted.

So I began to research again, think again, and pray again. The Lord again pointed me toward homeschooling. One afternoon, after volunteering, I talked to a beloved teacher at the public school. After she answered my questions, she leaned in and said, "Honey, get those sweet kids out of here." This dear older woman was full of kind words of encouragement for me and, as I left that day, she told me to keep them out of the schools in the older grades as well because the school atmosphere was volatile.

I was beginning to get excited and envision how our home would run if we moved ahead. As I was praying specifically about activities that would occupy the younger children while the older children did their school work, an acquaintance, who was a homeschooling mother of seven, made an unsolicited phone call to share her practical school day plan. Her call startled me for two reasons.

First, it was a direct and immediate answer to prayer. Second, we talked briefly about a news story that was just beginning to unfold from the west coast. It was April 20, 1999, and the news channels were reporting that two young men, fascinated by Goth culture, had walked into their school, Columbine High School near Littleton, Colorado, earlier that day and committed the worst school shooting in our nation's history, killing 13 and wounding more than 20 before turning the guns on themselves.

Interestingly, although I normally tend to be a fearful person, the shooting did not play a large role in my decision because I realized that evening that my choice had already been made. All things pointed toward homeschooling and the events of that day simply confirmed it.

> So whoever knows the right thing to do and fails to do it, for him it is sin. (James 4:17 ESV)

So, with my husband's agreement and what I discerned was the Lord's blessing, we began our adventure into this unknown world of having school at home.

Fast-forward almost two decades later and I find myself again wanting to cry. This time, however, I am not overwhelmed. I am wanting to cry because I am recalling all of the wonderful memories. The years are gone and the days have ended. The children are all moving on. The "babies" in the stroller are in college, the little girl hanging onto one side of the stroller is a registered nurse 2,500 miles from home and the little boy holding onto the other side of the stroller is earning his PhD and is the head of his own household. We praise God that all four of them know Jesus as Lord and Savior and my husband and I are grateful to call each one of them friend.

I say all of this to share my story, dear reader, not to say that God could not have saved my children or kept them out of trouble if we had done things differently. No, of course not. God is Sovereign.

> Blessed be the God and Father of our Lord Jesus Christ, who has blessed us in Christ, with every spiritual blessing in the heavenly places, even as he chose us in him before the foundation of the world, that we should be holy and blameless before him. In love he predestined us for adoption as sons through Jesus Christ, according to the purpose of his will, to the praise of his glorious grace, with which he has blessed us in the Beloved. (Ephesians 1:3–6 ESV)

Though armed with the truth and comfort that comes from God's word, please understand that the stakes are high. The judgments that you and your husband make for these young ones are crucial. They will compile your child's memories and life experiences. You have a unique opportunity to shape their little young lives in a way that no one else can. Paul Tripp, author, pastor and conference speaker, emphasizes an everlasting perspective toward parenting in his book "Forever" by stating:

> Eternity reminds parents that this life is not all there is. It sets before us the truth that this present life is not an ultimate destination for our kids, but a preparation for a final destination. The existence of forever forces parents to acknowledge the inescapable conclusion that life has consequences. Our actions and choices have a greater significance than their present results tell us. The choices we make, the investments we make, and the decisions that we make all have eternal consequences.[1]

Seek wisdom as you make education choices for your children. Seek the Lord's will for your family.

In his book "Bringing Up Boys" Dr. James Dobson, author, psychologist, and founder of Focus on the Family, tells of a Harvard University study that found that early bonding between mother and child is vital.

> Incredibly, 91 percent of college men who said they had not enjoyed a close relationship with their mothers developed coronary artery disease, hypertension, duodenal ulcers, and alcoholism by the midlife years.

> In short, Dr. Dobson goes on, the quality of early relationships between boys and their mothers is a powerful predictor of lifelong psychological and physical health.[2]

It is possible to enjoy a close relationship with your children if they attend school, but I think parents would be wise to recognize just how much they are missing during those eight to ten hours a day when their children are away and strongly consider having school at home.

Chapter 1

THE ESSENTIALS

> You shall love the Lord your God with all your heart and with all your soul and with all your might. And these words that I command you today shall be on your heart. You shall teach them diligently to your children, and shall talk of them when you sit in your house, and when you walk by the way, and when you lie down and when you rise.
>
> —Deuteronomy 6:5–7 ESV

I have a secret. Homeschooling can make your role as a Christian parent easier. Now before you throw this book out, let me explain.

One day our dryer had a malfunction with the moisture sensor and would turn off before the clothes were dry. If I pressed the button again, it would turn back on only to turn off again a few minutes later. Even though the dryer wasn't working properly, the dirty laundry continued to pile up, and family members still needed clean towels, washed clothes, and underwear. I was still responsible for doing the laundry, but my job was more difficult without the proper tools.

Your most important assignment as a Christian parent is to teach your children about God. You do not warrant salvation for your children, of course, because only God saves; but there is clear direction in scripture for parents to instruct their children in the ways of the Lord, tell of His might and grace, and engage them in honest and direct discussion. You are responsible for your children's training (Proverbs 22:6) and to some extent their actions (1 Samuel 2:12–36).

Practically speaking, if your children are away from home eight to ten hours a day, it can be very difficult to succeed at the job that has been entrusted to you as a Christian parent. It is as though you are trying to complete the task of teaching your children about God without the necessary tools—in this case, time.

The Bible records a time when an Egyptian pharaoh forced the captive Israelites to make bricks without the necessary ingredient—straw—and it was a serious hardship for them.

> The same day Pharaoh commanded the taskmasters of the people and their foremen, "You shall no longer give the people straw to make bricks, as in the past; let them go and gather straw for themselves. But the number of bricks that they made in the past you shall impose on them, you shall by no means reduce it, for they are idle. Therefore they cry, 'Let us go and offer sacrifice to our God.' Let heavier work be laid on the men that they may labor at it and pay no regard to lying words."

> So the taskmasters and the foremen of the people went out and said to the people, "Thus says Pharaoh, 'I will not give you straw. Go and get your straw yourselves wherever you can find it, but your work will not be reduced in the least'. So the people were scattered throughout all the land of Egypt to gather stubble for straw. The taskmasters were urgent saying, 'Complete your work, your daily task each day, as when there was straw.' (Exodus 5:6–13 ESV)

Raising godly children without all of the proper tools or ingredients can be difficult. I know because I trudged along that path for a couple of years when my children were in public school. I can remember sitting on our steps having a short devotion with them at the beginning of the day, and I can recall rushing to the church for children's choir after school, handing out snacks for the ride and leaving homework on the kitchen table to be tackled later that evening. In addition to the time constraints, the outside influences from being at school all day are strong, and the lessons introduced at the beginning and end of the day are comparatively short.

Your primary job as a Christian parent is to teach your children about God and homeschooling is an excellent tool that a parent can use to carry out this crucial responsibility.

But how? If I had to boil it all down, I believe that there are really just a couple of things that are truly essential in homeschooling. I will call them the big rocks of homeschooling. Our pastor once told us that if you put the big rocks in a jar first, all of the smaller rocks will fit, but if you put the smaller rocks in first, many times the big ones will not then fit. What are the essentials of homeschooling?

Big Rock 1—Give Your Children the Gospel

Simply having your children sit at the kitchen table and "do math" will not ensure that they will come to know Jesus as Lord and Savior. You must tell them. You must point out that God is holy but we are sinners. You must explain that Jesus came into our world and lived a perfect, sinless life, yet he died a sinner's death—the death that we as transgressors should rightfully die. You must describe Jesus's death and burial and explain that on the third day he rose up from the grave, defeating death and proving that He is God, the perfect one. You must declare to your children that if they repent of their sins, trust in Jesus, and accept His free gift of salvation, they will live with Him in heaven for all of eternity.

> And there is salvation in no one else, for there is no other name under heaven given among men by which we must be saved. (Acts 4:12 ESV)

According to Albert Mohler, president of the Southern Baptist Theological Seminary, believers must verbalize the gospel.

> The only way for the message of the gospel to be understood and believed is if it is articulated. In Romans 10, Paul teaches that the word that leads to faith has been brought near. This gospel word is powerful enough that all people everywhere can hear and believe the truth. Articulating the gospel is essentially and centrally verbal for people to become Christ followers.[1]

When we began our homeschooling adventure, I was not sure about all of the specifics. But I knew that the Lord did not want us to have school at home and merely slap a Christian label on it. I had a strong desire in my heart to introduce God to my children. I wanted them to know of His tender mercies and saving power. It was my first hope that they would all come to acknowledge Jesus as their Savior, be saved from hell, and be spared many of the sins that I embraced during my school years.

As I kept this goal in front of my eyes, I tried to incorporate God's truths into most everything we did. Please do not misunderstand. We certainly did not do this perfectly. Although I scheduled a Bible lesson for the beginning of every school day, occasionally it was set aside because something urgent presented an obstacle. Some days the kids didn't pay attention, some mornings the phone rang while we were praying, and at times one of us was grumpy or especially tired. But for the most part, we began our day with an age-appropriate Bible lesson, a song, and prayers.

We also tried to recognize "God moments" as they occurred. Some days, conversations would start up that were rich and deep, but off topic. These times can be the sweetest. I encourage you to recognize these moments as gifts from God and to seize them.

One example comes to my mind. Every day after lunch I would read out loud to the children. The books were usually on the academic level of the older students. Before I expected James and Melanie to comprehend, they were asked to sit with us and play quietly with a toy or draw a picture. I was often encouraged when one of them would draw a picture of a person or scene from the book that I was reading, which demonstrated an understanding of what was being conveyed. As I read, I would sometimes describe someone who was a professing Christian, but their life did not reflect this. When I spoke of that professing "Christian" I would make quotation marks in the air with my fingers. One day we were reading about a character, and James piped in by calling the character a bunny-eared Christian.

"A what?" I asked. "You know, a 'Christian,'" he said while making quotation marks, or bunny ears, with his little fingers. I was amused but also sobered.

What a wonderful opportunity to explain that people are not saved by works but only by Jesus. Christians are defined by Jesus's work, not by their own. Jesus paid it all! This was a perfect time to discuss the gospel, good and bad behavior, and perceiving the condition of someone's heart. I learned to (gulp) confess a judgmental attitude. This powerful lesson could not have been planned. It had to be taken as an unexpected gift.

Big Rock 2—Give Your Children Your Time

Spend time with your children. Lots and lots of time. There is no substitute or shortcut for this.

One of the most compelling appeals for spending time with your children that I have ever heard was given by Dr. Greg L. Bahnsen in a talk called "Christian Education as Covenant Faithfulness." The teaching on this audio spoke to my heart in a powerful way, and I would encourage anyone still on the fence about homeschooling to get a copy at Covenant Media Foundation. But there was one particular excerpt that especially got my attention.

> I'll ask you rhetorically. Are we diligently teaching our children to walk in covenant with God, to see everything through the filter of God's word, to evaluate everything according to the teaching of God's revelation, if we turn our children over to unbelieving teachers thirty hours a week, while we spend – probably – (it's a high estimate, but) four hours a week trying to instill in them the teaching

> of God's word? Thirty hours to the world, to a way of thinking that ignores God if not outright defies God, thirty hours a week for the world, four hours, maybe, at home and in church a week to counter balance that. Would you consider that – I mean if you were an employer – let's just put yourself in the position of the boss here. The boss says, I want you diligently to pursue the following project and then you told the boss – after he asked an accounting of you – well, what I did is I did thirty hours of other things and then four hours this week I pursued the project that you said I was to follow diligently. Do you think he would be pleased with your service?[2]

To give my children and their schooling the proper amount of attention I tried to limit my time on the phone or computer during the day. My goal was to think of homeschooling as my job and most of us would not sit at work and look at our phone or answer personal e-mails. I took the vocation of being a homeschooling mom seriously and strove to help our children realize how important they were to John and me and, ultimately, to God.

We also attempted to make the most of meal times by sitting together at the table for breakfast, lunch, and dinner, sharing food and conversation. For lunch it was normally just the kids and me; but, again, we sat at the table and had discussions.

At times sports or other activities threatened to infringe on our evening meal so I would often rearrange dinner time to accommodate a dance rehearsal or soccer practice; even if it meant having dinner as late as 8:30 or even 9:00. We tried to make mealtime a fun event and, while we did not always pull it off due to picky eaters or grumpy days, we all really came to value these times. Even now, we all enjoy being together for meals when we can.

We also utilized drive time for building relationships as John and I carted them back and forth to their activities. Some of the sweetest conversations were during times in the van. Some disagreements occurred there too. The kids used to tease us when we had a particularly difficult time getting out of the house and were all packed in the vehicle by exclaiming sarcastically that they were so happy to be having family time.

Big Rock 3 – Give Your Children Critical Thinking Skills

At the end of their schooling your children will not know everything. Certainly, you and I do not know everything! But at the end of their schooling, they should hopefully have many of the tools that they will need to think critically and discern truth from falsehood.

Frankly, this fallen world is a rough place where Christian beliefs and values are ridiculed and maligned. It is very important for Christian parents to equip their children with critical thinking skills. In our family we did this in four ways.

First, we encouraged our children to be voracious readers and, as they got older, we assigned material with differing viewpoints for reading and discussion.

Second, we often discussed sensitive topics such as racism, politics, sex, creation and morality, just to name a few.

Third, during high school, we went through a worldview course together called "Understanding the Times" by Summit Ministries where we looked in-depth at competing ideas and philosophies.

Fourth, we encouraged our children to participate in a rigorous speech and debate organization called the National Christian Forensics and Communications Association (NCFCA) whose mission "is to promote excellence in communications through competitive opportunities where homeschool students develop the skills necessary to think critically and communicate effectively in order to address life issues from a biblical worldview in a manner that glorifies God."[3]

As my children researched, wrote and delivered speeches on various topics such as the history of dialects, the importance of prayer, the lives and contributions of Augustine and hymn writer Fanny Crosby, they polished their writing and public speaking skills. As they participated in the interpretative speech category they memorized large passages from great books such as "Pilgrim's Progress" and "The Hiding Place" acting out scenes for a panel of judges who ranked and critiqued them.

As they participated in debate they learned to develop and articulate both sides of an intellectual argument. They were able to present their evidence and logical conclusions on themes such as freedom over equity or due process over the discovery of fact. In this way, they sharpened their much-needed critical thinking skills in a fun but extremely competitive environment.

We were part of NCFCA for over a decade and put more miles on our van than I can count as we traveled from Tennessee (where we now live), to Tulsa, Oklahoma, Minneapolis, Minnesota, Baton Rouge, Louisiana, and many places in between. We made friends all around the nation and, during the years when we were involved, I witnessed my children grow from young, apprehensive, and self-conscious public speakers to national competitors.

Winning is, of course, a lot of fun, but rich character traits were honed when their names weren't called; when they didn't win. The temptation to criticize the judges or make excuses crouched near both the students and the parents; but opportunities to trust God, congratulate the opponent, and remember that your worth can only be found in Jesus abounded.

If you ask my children about their experience with NCFCA today, they would tell you that this was the most effective activity we ever undertook. In fact, Melanie, now a sophomore in college, was assigned a speech in one of her classes and I sent her a text mid-morning asking how it went. She responded with the following:

> I think it went really well! I'm so thankful we did (speech and debate) all those years. It prepared me not only to wake up and get dressed in a suit, but also for speaking and critical thinking. Soooo important![4]

Yes, these activities take a lot of time, particularly NCFCA, and not all families can fully participate; but sitting at your kitchen table discussing weighty matters or forming a local debate group that meets in your home once a month is doable. We, as Christian parents, must help our children sharpen their critical thinking skills because the dissolute ideas that await them in college and beyond are ubiquitous and consequential.

Chapter 2

THE HOME IN HOMESCHOOLING

> She looks well to the ways of her household and does not eat the bread of idleness. Her children rise up and call her blessed; her husband also, and he praises her.
>
> —Proverbs 31:27–28 ESV

My favorite spot in our home is on our screened-in porch. This magnificent treehouse-mimicking enclosure has been the venue for Bible studies, personal devotions, pleasure reading, schooling, both casual and life-changing conversations, and the harbor where our family has come together and shared thousands of meals.

One fall day as I was sitting on my porch among the beauty of the changing leaves, I noticed a large piece of plastic stuck up in a tree behind our house. Apparently, some packing material had blown into our neighbor's yard and was impossible to remove from this very tall tree. Due to the location of the tree, it was doubtful that our neighbors could even see it. Yet, day after day I eyed this large piece of trash and as the autumn leaves began to drop, it become more and more glaring to me. This piece of garbage was threatening to steal my joy!

Some of my homeschooling days seemed a lot like sitting in my favorite spot in our home, but not enjoying it because I was focusing on a piece of plastic in a tree. The one thing that was not ideal would threaten to steal the joy from all of the things that were going well.

Realize that there will be things about homeschooling that are not perfect. We live in a fallen world and we live among sinners. Your curricula will not be perfect, your children will not behave wonderfully and your days will not flow seamlessly. Resist the urge to focus on the negative and instead look at what *is* good – being at home all day with the ones you love and teaching them about God's amazing creation.

Create an Atmosphere of Love and Joy

Moms are in a unique position in the family because they will usually have the greatest effect on the mood of the home. You, as the woman of the house, can choose to create an atmosphere of love and acceptance or one of nagging and defeat.

> The wisest of women builds her house, but folly with her own hands tears it down.
> (Proverbs 14:1 ESV)

Whether you have decided to homeschool, are still gathering information, or even end up sending your children to school, I encourage you to give your family the incredible gift of a loving home. This, of course, can only be accomplished through the power of the Holy Spirit, so ask Him to help you. Christian homes should be sanctuaries where members find love and acceptance. For the homeschooling family, it can be even more important because being in the home among family members is so very constant.

Love your children. Enjoy your children. Have fun with your children. Make sweet memories. Sit on the porch, eat popsicles, and talk. Share their interests. Invite them to share some of yours. Display wisdom by taking every opportunity that God gives you to point them to the Savior.

I know the days seem long, but, as my husband often says, the years are short. You have such a brief season to shape their lives. Be willing to set aside some of your time and preferences for just that. You will be very glad you did.

Organize Your Home

As I began to contemplate our new way of life and how homeschooling would look for us, I spent some time organizing our home. I decided that our school would primarily be contained in the main part of the house so that I could oversee school work and at the same time put chicken or beef in the crock pot or oven, peel potatoes or prepare other vegetables, and even fold laundry.

I moved a shelf near the kitchen table to be used for books and supplies, and I set up a playroom in the living room that was around the corner from the kitchen. At the time, it worked out great because we had more toys than furniture. I hung maps on the walls, placed a globe on the shelf, and arranged a basket of "free reading" books in the family room. I also brought a large white board up from the basement and put it in a corner of the dining room.

I gave our entire house a deep cleaning and made room in the drawers and closets for extra notebooks and supplies. I moved our picnic table into the sun, cleaned off the deck and, finally, stocked the van with training CDs so we could learn while running errands.

Devise A Chore Schedule

I devised a chore chart giving everyone a set of jobs. Frankly, this was a challenge for me because I found it easier to just do the chores rather than teach young children to complete these assignments. But, I realized that it is good for children to be a part of the work force in the home - making them, hopefully, feel like an essential part of the family. I also surmised that teaching them to do these chores would be better for all of us in the long run. It was.

Discipline Those You Love

I also tightened up on my discipline. Our children were generally well-behaved and we had been addressing most disobedience issues immediately so we did not have a tremendous amount of work to do; but I had to admit that occasionally I overlooked behaviors that should have been corrected. Sometimes I made excuses for my children and sometimes I was just a little lazy.

As I prepared for having my children at home with me all day again, I made some slight adjustments. I was surprised to see how straightforward it was to simply address and correct the improper behaviors or attitudes and, as a result, our home ran better and we were all more productive. It was also better for our souls.

> For the moment all discipline seems painful rather than pleasant, but later it yields the peaceful fruit of righteousness to those who have been trained by it. (Hebrews 12:11 ESV)

I encourage you to take a little time before you begin homeschooling to address the poor behaviors and crummy attitudes that you observe. You may need to explain the rules more clearly or you may need to begin a new system. You may even need to apologize to your children for not pointing things out sooner.

When taking disciplinary action, it is crucial that you broach the subject with a heart to benefit your child. What are the behaviors and demeanors that really need addressing? Will changing these habits be better for the child or simply make your day a little less of a hassle? As Tedd Tripp explains in his book "Shepherding a Child's Heart", "You have no biblical obligation to censure your children for everything they do that is irritating to you."[1]

Dr. James Dobson frequently points out in his books and lectures that childish irresponsibility, such as spilling or losing something, acting silly in the living room and breaking an expensive china cup, or leaving his or her bike out in the rain is inevitable and should be addressed with a gracious, gentle tone.[2]

Willful disobedience, Dobson clarifies, should be addressed with a firmer hand, but without exasperating the child. Dobson explains that a parent should have control in their home, but should not give in to anger. Angry parental outbursts do not work, Dobson contends, and illustrates with the following:

> … imagine yourself tearing through a school zone one morning on the way to the office. You suddenly look in the rearview mirror and see a black-and-white squad car bearing down on you from behind. Eight red lights are flashing and the siren is screaming. The officer uses his loudspeaker to tell you to pull over to the curb. When you have stopped, he opens

> his door and approaches your window. He is six foot nine, has a voice like the Lone Ranger's, and wears a big gun on his hip. His badge is gleaming in the light. He is carrying a little leather-bound book of citations that you have seen before—last month. The officer speaks politely but firmly, 'Sir, I have you on radar traveling sixty-five miles per hour in a twenty-mile-per-hour zone. May I see your driver's license, please?' The officer doesn't scream, cry, or criticize you. He doesn't have to.[3]

The home is where so much growth takes place and, sadly, where hearts can be bruised. I encourage you to pray for your home and the precious souls living there and liberally ask God for help.

> By wisdom a house is built, and by understanding it is established; by knowledge the rooms are filled with all precious and pleasant riches. (Proverbs 24:3–4 ESV)

Chapter 3

THE SCHOOL IN HOMESCHOOLING

All your children shall be taught by the Lord, and great shall be the peace of your children.

—Isaiah 54:13 ESV

"Put your books down; it's time to go to school," I called out from the kitchen where I was packing lunches. "Let's go" I urged as Brett and Kim crawled out from under their warm blankets on the two sofas where they were happily reading. We walked out into the cold, dark early morning and headed to the local school where they stood in line to get inside, shuffled to their classrooms to listen to announcements, participated in roll call and got settled in. Almost two hours passed before they got back to the books.

Time efficiency and convenience were not the reasons I chose homeschooling, but they were delightful by-products. As we began to homeschool, our lives became simpler. The children were able to stay up a little later, sleep a little later, and (in the younger grades) complete their school work a little earlier. Our days were more efficient and, frankly, even though I am not an intellectual by any means, the education my children received at home was superior to what they were getting from one of the most esteemed counties in the nation. They read more, explored more, and understood more, and their test scores proved it.

Many don't realize it, but school at home is not a new idea. Most of us just assume government schools have been around forever, but it has actually been less than 100 years that American children have been required to attend school in this nation.

> Massachusetts passed the first compulsory school laws in 1852. New York followed the next, and by 1918, all American children were required to attend at least elementary school.[1]

So, as you begin to set up a school in your home, realize that you are certainly not the first American to take on the task.

> Hundreds of years ago, most learning happened at home. Parents taught their children, or, if their families could afford, private tutors did the job.[2]

You are not alone. Currently there are approximately 2.3 million homeschoolers in the nation.[3]

Begin With Prayer

As you inaugurate the school in your home, the best thing you can do for your household (or anything else for that matter) is to commit your endeavor to the Lord. Spend time with God, asking him to prepare your heart and mind for the task in front of you. What is the Almighty's vision for your homeschool? How does He want to shape and mold your children?

Have Mentors

People are usually willing to talk to others about their profession. It is the same with homeschooling moms. Most of us are not only willing, but eager to share our experiences.

One of the first things I did as a homeschooling mom was to seek out ladies in my church who were a little ahead of me in this undertaking and ask them questions. What subject do you do first? What do you do with the younger children while you are helping with the math? When do you clean your house?

One friend was very gracious and allowed me to come over and observe her morning. I arrived at their home with bagels and cream cheese and, after a brief greeting and explanation of why I was there to her young daughter, I simply sat in the background and watched. I learned so much that day. I was surprised at how unimposing the schooling was in their home. Her student simply sat at the kitchen table and worked on math, grammar and spelling while my friend held her baby in one arm and unloaded the dishwasher and did other chores with the other. Then, she explained, after the baby goes down for a nap she and her student would read. She walked me over and showed me the place where she and her daughter snuggled up together with their books.

That morning made a big impression on me, not only because it looked doable, but (more importantly), because hers was a home with a warm atmosphere. The children were cared for and loved. Their home seemed to have an abundance of joy and I wanted that for our home. I realized that day that the books and lessons are important, but a home that displays respect for those living there and honor to Jesus Christ is, as the American Express commercial states, priceless.

The answers to those other questions? You have the freedom to do what works for you in your home. I learned that some moms complete the most challenging subjects in the morning and save art and pleasure reading for the afternoon. Some homeschools encourage the completion of all of their academics in the morning to allow for chores and sports in the afternoon. Some homes have a separate school room; others require the students to complete their lessons at the kitchen table. Some moms require their children to rise early, get dressed, make their beds, have breakfast, and begin their studies before 8:00 am. Other homes have a more casual atmosphere and students can be found still in their pajamas at 11:00. The point is that, in your homeschool, you and your husband get to decide. You will find that the mentors you interact with will give you a lot of possibilities to consider.

Have a Plan

Through the years, I have discovered that the main key to planning is to have one.

> Where there is no vision, the people perish; but he
> that keepeth the law, happy is he.
> (Proverbs 29:18 KJV)

The summer before we started formerly homeschooling I began to really think about time management. What time should we eat breakfast? Realistically, what time should we start our school work? Should math class, for instance, be over at a certain time with any uncompleted work being done in the child's free time? Should I read out loud to the children right after we eat lunch or should we do the dishes first? So many questions popped up.

But after thinking it through and compiling my plan, I wrote up our schedule clearly on a large piece of poster board and put it on the kitchen wall. Amazingly, the kids did not argue with the schedule. If it was written on the poster board they just seemed to acquiesce and abide by it. For instance, if one child asked for a snack I would point to the board and explain that it was not yet time for a snack. Astonishingly, they accepted the answer most of the time. My husband and I would laugh about it privately wondering if we should put everything on the "magic poster board". I just think that most children seem to thrive when there is structure.

Allow for Some Free Time

Be willing to set your schedule aside occasionally for a field trip or a day at the water park, but, for the most part, I realized, it serves everyone better if most days are filled with school work and planned activities even if the planned activity is *free time*. Free time with parameters, such as no electronics, can be a wonderful occasion for the child to use his or her imagination. What a child does in his or her free time can also show a parent where the child's interests lie. Does he take apart and fix things, construct towns and cities with Legos or blocks, write in a journal, listen to music, dance, or ask to cook? Engineer, architect, designer, writer, musician, critic, dancer, performer, or cook?

Answering Critics

In the early days of my homeschooling efforts I was obsessed with what others thought of us. I desperately wanted people to see the benefits of what we were doing and think well of us, more particularly, me. As I look back on those days I can see the sinfulness of my own heart because, even though I knew God called me to school my children at home, I cared so much about the perception of others that I kept questioning and even doubting Him. One day I stumbled onto the following verse:

> For they loved the glory that comes from man more than the glory that comes from God.
> (John 12:43 ESV)

That verse described me. I had been desiring man's praise and approval. After I realized and confessed my sin, I endeavored to lay down my craving for the accolades of others and rest in the Lord. That was good for my soul.

The truth is that there will be critics and the best response to criticism is to simply school and care for your children day after day. Sit in the sun and read to them while they eat ice cream, give them their math assignments and grade their essays. Give spelling quizzes and show them how to be kind to others. Encourage them to memorize Bible verses. Answer the critics by homeschooling your children, simply homeschooling your children.

Dave Ramsey, businessman, author, radio and television personality, motivational speaker, and creator of Financial Peace University, a biblically based financial training series, tells a story of asking a prosperous billionaire for advice on becoming successful and the suggestion of this fortuitous man was to read a particular book. Dave Ramsey relays the story like this:

> His second suggestion was to read a book that he guaranteed would change my life. I'm a huge reader, so I was really excited about this idea. I had my pen to the paper, ready to write down the name of this transformational book.

> 'Dave, have you ever read The Tortoise and the Hare?' he asked. Huh? A fairy tale? What's that got to do with wealth?
>
> Seeing the weird look on my face, my friend said, 'Dave, we live in a world full of rabbits. Everybody is running around, hopping here and there without paying attention to where they're going. If you want to succeed, you've got to stay focused and move slow and steady.'
>
> Then he leaned in and hit me with the clincher: 'Every time I read that book, the tortoise wins.'
>
> I think Solomon was making a similar point in Proverbs 21:5. Diligence requires patience and perseverance. It's much more tortoise than hare.[4]

It is the same principle whether it is gaining wealth or knowledge. Slow and steady. As you are faithful to teach your children day by day, year by year, they will learn. Their character will be molded. They will master the skill of sharing with others under your watchful eye, they will witness the importance of being a part of a family, and they will grow into decent adults. Hopefully, by God's grace, they will come to know Jesus as Lord and Savior and, of course, learn to read, write, add and subtract along the way.

There may indeed come a time when you actually do have to answer a critic with words and I encourage you to look carefully at each situation. Is your critic a well-meaning grandparent or beloved friend or is it a busybody neighbor? The family member or dear friend who loves you and your children most likely deserves a well thought through explanation and may have some valid points for consideration. The busybody neighbor or acquaintance may need to be told kindly that you and your husband have things under control. As you answer your critics you will want to ask your husband to step in so that the two of you can present a united team.

Be Humble and Accountable

While you do not want to be beholden to someone else's opinion, you should not discount your own sin nature and be willing to ask for feedback. Just like anyone else, we homeschooling moms can become lazy, proud, or foolish, and just like anyone else we should desire and ask for accountability. Ideally, your husband is the best choice, but if he does not want to take on that role, perhaps a close friend or relative would be a good option. Ask for honest feedback. This will take humility.

It will also take humility on your part to see a nugget of truth even in unfriendly criticism. An unfavorable stance can actually make you work harder or even draw attention to a legitimate point.

For example, one evening at a children's program at church I was checking my kids in and noticed a young boy, approximately ten years old, in front of us signing himself in. The woman at the table asked for his address, but he did not know it. She asked for his phone number, but he did not know that either and finally she asked for the name of his school and he mumbled that he was homeschooled. The woman looked annoyed and rolled her eyes. I don't know why God allowed me to witness this exchange because, up until this point, I had always heard about and seen exemplary behavior and extensive knowledge from homeschoolers, but in an odd sort of way that evening I was humbled. I took it as a warning to make sure my children obtained necessary life skills and I made sure they knew their address and phone number on the way home that evening!

Stay humble and accountable. Allow God to teach you, by using His word and other people, and instruct your children, through you.

Know the Law

Another important item to check off your list as you prepare to begin homeschooling is to find out what the law in your state requires and comply with it.

As you desire to adhere to the law it may be a good idea for you to join the Home School Legal Defense Association (HSLDA). We are life-time members and have found their organization to be a wonderful resource and insurance policy of sorts. HSLDA provides current information to members concerning specific laws in their state and will represent a family member in court if there should ever be a legal problem. They also update their members regularly on instances where the state overstepped its boundaries and trampled a family's right to educate their children at home. Whether you join HSLDA or research the rules on your own, it is extremely important that you comply with the homeschool law in your state.

An example of submitting to authorities and the law is given in the following biblical narrative:

> But Daniel resolved that he would not defile himself with the king's food, or with the wine that he drank. Therefore he asked the chief of the eunuchs to allow him not to defile himself. And God gave Daniel favor and compassion in the sight of the chief of the eunuchs, and the chief of the eunuchs said to Daniel, "I fear my lord the king, who assigned your food and your drink; for why should he see that you were in worse condition than the youths who are

of your own age? So you would endanger my head with the king." Then Daniel said to the steward whom the chief of the eunuchs had assigned over Daniel, Hananiah, Mishael, and Azariah, "Test your servants for ten days; let us be given vegetables to eat and water to drink. Then let our appearance and the appearance of the youths who eat the king's food be observed by you, and deal with your servants according to what you see." So he listened to them in this matter, and tested them for ten days. At the end of ten days it was seen that they were better in appearance and fatter in flesh than all the youths who ate the king's food. So the steward took away their food and the wine they were to drink, and gave them vegetables.

As for these four youths, God gave them learning and skill in all literature and wisdom, and Daniel had understanding in all visions and dreams. At the end of the time, when the king had commanded that they should be brought in, the chief of the eunuchs brought them in before Nebuchadnezzar. And the king spoke with them, and among all of them none was found like Daniel, Hananiah, Mishael, and Azariah. Therefore they stood before the king. And in every matter of wisdom and understanding about which the king inquired of them, he found them ten times better than all the magicians and enchanters that were in all his kingdom. And Daniel was there until the first year of King Cyrus. (Daniel 1:8-21 ESV)

Testing

The above biblical narrative also speaks to testing. We have homeschooled in three different states and all of them required yearly or bi-yearly examinations. Some years, I sent our children to a local church where they tested with a group of students who were overseen by a facilitator or proctor. Other years, living in a different state, I was able to test our children myself in our home. Again, state laws differ so you need to check the particulars in your state. Testing can be nerve racking, but can also be a wonderful tool to let you know how your children are doing.

Testing can also give your children a wonderful opportunity to excel. According Dr. Brian Ray of the National Home Education Research Institute, homeschooled students score typically 15 to 30 percentile points above public school students on standardized achievement tests.[5]

Although I nervously paced up and down the halls of a local church when my children were first being tested, their scores were very good. I am happy to report that their scores only got better the longer we homeschooled.

Chapter 4

CHOOSING CURRICULA

> See to it that no one takes you captive by philosophy and empty deceit, according to human tradition, according to the elemental spirits of the world, and not according to Christ.
>
> —Colossians 2:8 ESV

"How can I possibly make these choices?" I wondered, as I walked from booth to booth in the huge hotel conference center. My friend and I had traveled almost 90 miles to attend this homeschool gathering where vendors educate and convince their potential customers and knowledgeable speakers hold seminars on a variety of homeschooling topics. This was a world that, until then, I did not even know existed and here I was right in the middle of it. How could I choose?

I feel a little silly about it now, but that day, feeling very confused and even a little lightheaded, I left the large conference room to go out in the hall, sit on a bench, and breathe deeply. "Lord, can I really do this?" I prayed silently. "I have no idea what I am doing!"

I did not actually purchase anything that day, which I think was a good thing. I observed, asked questions, and tried to learn as much as I could in that one short day. My inexperience did not last long, however, and the next time I attended a similar convention I walked confidently up to the booths with direct, thoughtful questions just like a seasoned homeschooling mom.

Your knowledge, too, will come and you will be able to make wonderful choices for your family. Remember, how you felt when you brought your first little baby home from the hospital? You were probably pretty scared. But soon, you had that young one propped up on your hip holding him or her expertly with your right arm and confidently pushing a vacuum cleaner or performing some other task with the left. Be encouraged as you search and assured that there are creative and interesting ways to introduce your children to the wonders of God's creation. I am confident that there is a plan that will serve your family well.

Who Are You?

Before making your purchases, I would encourage you to be honest with yourself about yourself. What and how much are you realistically able to do? If a curriculum sounds wonderful, but requires you to read to your children all day and you have nine children at home, that might not be the best choice for your family right now. Or perhaps you can modify it to fit with your lifestyle. If a curriculum is heavy on worksheets and your students are four young wiggly boys, that might not be the one for this particular academic year.

Be realistic about your style. Are you the type of mom who enjoys facilitating science experiments? Do you love good books? Do you want to explain math problems on a white or chalk board or would you prefer that your children simply watch a video explanation? Will you be comfortable grading their writing assignments or would you like to trade off with a friend or even send your child to another instructor for that subject?

You will also want to take your children's learning styles and personalities into account as you make the best choices for your family.

The upside of having all of these options is that there is usually something for everyone. Many cities hold homeschool conventions like the one my friend and I attended where you can get a good hands-on look at curricula and learn from the great lectures and symposiums.

Ask Your Mentors

You will definitely want to talk to your mentors. They will perhaps even allow you to look at their books. Again, most people love to talk about what they do. Perhaps you could ask older children in your church about their school work, after obtaining their parent's permission, of course. Realize that no curriculum is perfect so be sure to ask about the pros and cons.

Utilize the Home School Legal Defense Association

I mention HSLDA again because it is such a helpful organization. On their website is a plethora of up-to-date information, both general and specific, about homeschooling and curricula choices.

Other Instructors

Occasionally, you may prefer to have an outside teacher for your child. Perhaps you feel ill-equipped to teach a particular subject or your child seems to need some extra accountability for a short season. Perhaps the whole family simply thrives better when one day in your week is just a little different from the others. Observe your children and be willing to give them what you and your husband think that they need.

One option to consider is joining a local cooperative or co-op. A homeschool co-op is a group of homeschooling families who come together to enhance their homeschooling experience by sharing in the education of their children.[1] You may teach a subject that you have mastered while another parent teaches information that you do not know. Some groups require families to pay so that the group can hire teachers instead. Some co-ops are a combination of both. Each co-op is obviously structured differently, but there is often one that will meet the needs of your family. Ask your mentors or friends about co-ops in your area.

Another possibility to explore is an online school where you can enroll your child for just a class or two.

If you have a community college nearby, they will often allow high school students to attend a couple of classes if they meet the specified criteria, such as achieving a certain score on a standardized test. As a parent, you will want to discern whether your child is mature enough for the experience, of course, both academically and spiritually, before enrolling.

If you cannot afford these options, perhaps you can ask your husband to take over one of the classes or trade off with a friend.

What Did We Use?

Every family is different, the needs of individual households are diverse and you have the freedom to provide books and curricula that serves your needs and the needs of your husband and children. Having said that, I do recognize that specifics can be helpful, especially in the beginning. I am delighted to provide our personal preferences with the following caveat: Our family is probably different than yours.

Naming Names

I began teaching my children at home using the **Calvert Education Program**. **Calvert** was simple to use and academically rigorous, two factors I highly valued. The entire program came to our home in a cardboard box complete with supplies.

I used **Calvert** with my oldest twins for two years, but, discontinued it for two reasons. One, it was comparatively expensive and, secondly, it is a secular program. At the time, consumers were required to purchase the entire curriculum. It included a science program that, as a Christian, I found objectionable, so I decided to research other options. **Calvert** now offers the opportunity to purchase individual classes.

The Choices Are Yours

After those first two years I began to use a variety of curricula. Remember that you and your husband are in charge of your homeschool and, if necessary, you can modify how you use the material or even change the curricula. It is okay.

Bible

> Train up a child in the way he should go; even when he is old he will not depart from it. (Proverbs 22:6 ESV)

At first I taught our Bible class, but after a couple of years my husband started leading this special time. We started out using beautiful pictures or flash-a-cards that we purchased from **A Beka Books**. We would ask one child to hold up the picture while my husband or I read the corresponding passage from scripture. Then we would sing along with the music from excellent song books, such as "Hymns for a Kid's Heart" by Bobbie Wolgemuth and Joni Eareckson Tada. We would end our Bible time by praying together.

As the children grew older, we began using **Sonlight's** Bible curriculum where a daily Bible reading and a passage from a Christian book was required. There were questions at the end of the lesson for the children to answer in a notebook.

When our youngest twins were in the elementary grades we would simply modify the assignments by asking them to just listen as the biblical passage was discussed each morning. As they grew older they, of course, joined in with the work load.

In the later years, when the kids were more accomplished musicians, we added live music. John, my husband, would end our mornings by leading us in prayer.

Language Arts/English

We used a variety of curricula including **Sonlight** for grammar and dictation**, A Beka Books** for sentence diagramming, and **Spelling**

Power by Beverly Adams-Gordon for spelling assignments. We rounded out our language arts program for the lower grades by having the children practice their penmanship skills by copying Bible verses as assigned by Carol Ann Retzer in her series entitled **A Reason for Handwriting**. The children colored the pictures at the top of their worksheets and we hung them on the wall for decoration and memorization.

For high school we used **SMARR Publishers** for excellent reading and writing assignments, **Classical Roots** by Norma Fifer and Nancy Flowers to broaden their understanding of the English language, and **Analogies** by Arthur Liebman to sharpen their communication skills. For vocabulary we used both **Wordly Wise** workbooks, published by EPS Literacy and Intervention, and **The Words You Should Know**, by David Olsen, which is a book filled with just that – words you should know. Each week, I would choose several words to pronounce and define and on Fridays I would give a quiz. Each week I would add more words, but would continue quizzing them on the previous words to keep them fresh in their minds.

Math

For my younger twins I started them out using math workbooks from **A Beka Books,** surmising that one colorful sheet taken out of a workbook would be much less daunting than an entire math book placed in front of them each day. They enjoyed completing their cheerful math paper and would often ask for another one to work on before the morning was over, which was something I never anticipated.

After arriving at the third grade level, the children began using **Saxon Math**. **Saxon** is not all that exciting, but it is an excellent program that does not allow your student to forget old concepts when new ones are introduced because the old concepts are continuously revisited. For the older grades (middle school and up), I added the **Digital Interactive Video Education** that corresponded with the **Saxon** program. After completing the entire **Saxon** program through Calculus, two of our children successfully completely higher math classes at a local community college while still in high school.

Science

> The heavens declare the glory of God, and the sky above proclaims his handiwork.
> (Psalm 19:1 ESV)

For the younger grades, I taught the science classes using **Apologia**, which has a Christian worldview. We had a lot of fun doing the experiments out on the deck and, because I am not really a science person, I sometimes watched in amazement as the experiments actually worked. Sometimes, we watched them fail and I would say, "Well, let's go inside and talk about what was supposed to happen."

Eventually we supplemented their science requirements. The older twins attended a co-op for Biology and Chemistry, where they continued using **Apologia**. For Physics, we hired a pre-medical student to teach from **Apologia's** curriculum in our basement. I invited three other teens to join the class to make it more worthwhile for the young instructor, who did a superb job, and my teens enjoyed a fresh perspective and also some time with their friends. For Advanced Biology and Chemistry, we sent them to the local community college.

When the time came for the younger twins to take Biology, I hired my oldest daughter, a nursing student at the time, to instruct. We spread newspapers on the kitchen table and Kim supervised the dissection of the animals from a kit that I purchased from **Apologia**. I would smile as I would overhear Kim tell them that she would take away points if they did not do their lab report correctly. Although she was tough on her younger siblings (expecting them to have the skills of college students), they all enjoyed the experience.

History

I began using **Sonlight** for history because there is a lot of required reading and my children love to read. We continued using **Sonlight** for history, studying World, American, Eastern Hemisphere, Church, Twentieth Century World, and American Government, because the books are really, really good. We often found ourselves discussing them at the lunch table and my children did not begrudge the work. It was enjoyable for all of us.

Sonlight is an excellent program, but, in addition to a lot of reading, it also requires a significant amount of parental involvement, particularly in the younger years. The program is quite different from "regular school" in that there are not many tests or worksheets, but a lot of reading and discussing.

Audiobooks

Because our family did so much reading for both English and History we sometimes incorporated the help of **LibriVox**, *"a group of world-wide volunteers who read and record public domain texts creating free public domain audiobooks for download from their website and other digital library hosting sites on the internet."*[2] Each of us could listen to a book recording and then come together several times a week to discuss the material. **LibriVox** currently has over 10,000 audiobooks for free access so the classics are almost always available.[3]

Current Events

We normally discussed news topics at meals and, when the kids got to be high school aged, I would require them to come to lunch twice a week with two news items to discuss, one domestic and one foreign. I usually didn't critique the topics they selected, allowing them a lot freedom to choose what they wanted to research. Their material swept from politics to foreign affairs, over to a severe weather event or a football game, to technology or even fashion. If they could not come up with anything at all, however, I would require a short written essay on two events that would be due later that afternoon. The threat of a writing assignment in lieu of a casual oral discussion usually dissuaded arriving at the lunch table with nothing to examine. Of course, my husband and I would bring them up to date on important news events as they happened.

Computer Science

Two of our children took an online computer class through **Keystone** High School. The class was challenging and interesting and, even though my husband was available to answer their questions, they were able to do most of the work without additional instruction.

What Else?

In addition to the core classes I used the following curricula with our high schoolers:

Economics: Economics in a Box by Pam Cooper
Health and Wellness: Total Health by Susan Boe
Foreign Language (German and Spanish) Rosetta Stone
ARTistic Pursuits by Brenda Ellis
Personal Finance: Financial Peace by Dave Ramsey
Worldview: Understanding the Times through Summit Ministries
Driver's Ed in a Box by Patrick L. Barrett

Biblical Greek

Sometimes it can be a little more challenging to find exactly what you're looking for and you may have to go in a little different direction than the one you were planning. Our challenge came with a foreign language. I just assumed that our children would fulfill their foreign language requirement with a pretty common language; but our son, James, became interested in learning Biblical Greek. I did some research, but the foreign language programs I was familiar with didn't offer biblical languages so I began asking around in the homeschooling community.

Soon I discovered two families who were in the process of forming a small class about eighty minutes from our home. This small group was to be instructed by a biblical languages graduate student using **Basics of Biblical Greek** by William D. Mounce and, even though I didn't plan for this, the benefits seemed to outweigh the costs so we signed James up and were not disappointed. Through the experience, James learned Biblical Greek under the direction of a man who is now a pastor and made some lasting friendships with young men who are serious about God's word.

God even redeemed the weekly two-and-a-half-hour commute because James was learning to drive and was able to practice on a portion of the highway that was less congested than the section near our home. It was a blessing for James and me to hang out together and talk during what came to be our sweet weekly time in the van. We thanked God for that class many times and it is a now a fond memory for us.

Biblical Hebrew

James was also interested in furthering this area of study by taking Biblical Hebrew. When we asked the same graduate student for options he agreed to continue teaching, this time giving private lessons using **Basics of Biblical Hebrew** by Gary D. Pratico and Miles V. Van Pelt. Instead of meeting face to face, they utilized Skype. Each week the instructor would teach the lesson and assign the work and the following week he would go over any problems before teaching a new lesson. It worked out really well. The instructor earned some extra money and James learned the language and also deepened their friendship and mentoring relationship.

A Lot of Choices

There are many options and a lot of different ways of doing things. Continue to ask God for direction and keep your eyes open for answers. God provided so graciously to us throughout the years that I began to trust that if He did not provide it we simply must not need it.

> All I have needed Thy hand hath provided – 'Great is Thy faithfulness," Lord, unto me!

Chapter 5

LIFE IN THE MIDDLE OF YOUR SCHOOL

> The thief comes only to steal and kill and destroy. I (Jesus) came that they may have life and have it abundantly.
>
> —John 10:10 ESV

"What is your life verse?" the hostess asked as I walked into her home for a going away party for our friend. She pointed me to a small table where a Bible and a highlighter awaited my declaration. As I flipped through the Bible, noticing the markings that the others had left for our departing friend, the hostess explained that a life verse is simply a favorite Bible verse that offers inspiration. "What is my favorite verse? All of them", I wanted to say. "It's the Bible!"

But then I thought back to the time that, as a brand new Christian, I felt like God actually spoke to me through His word. I was at a Bible study and the instructor read the following verse,

> I will restore to you the years that the swarming locust has eaten, the hopper, the destroyer and the cutter, my great army, which I sent among you. (Joel 2:25 ESV)

As I heard that verse for the very first time, years ago, my heart jumped and I knew that God was speaking, through His word, directly to my newly believing heart. "Oh God", I prayed silently, "Will you indeed restore the years the locust – sin – has demolished"?

As I stood at my friend's party, pondering a life verse, I realized that the Lord had indeed restored the years. Sin had eaten parts of my life, but God had repaired the broken places and made my life beautiful. He had forgiven me and washed me with His blood. By His grace our marriage was thriving, our children knew their Savior, and I was learning more and more about the Lord's amazing grace each day. That obscure verse, in the second chapter of Joel, was indeed my life verse and my sentiments are exemplified further in the words of the song, "Beautiful", by Dennis Cleveland:

Beautiful, beautiful
Jesus is beautiful,
And Jesus makes beautiful
Things of my life.
Carefully touching me,
Causing my eyes to see,
Jesus makes beautiful
Things of my life.[1]

As you teach and train your children at home each day, you will also be living life. Your children will be living life. Although your days may get chaotic, try to think of each day as a gift. Homeschooling should ideally not be thought of as a burden, but as a present to be opened and enjoyed each day.

As I reflect on savoring the moments of life I think about my friend, Kara, who had a massive heart attack right after the birth of their fifth child. Kara survived the ordeal and, although she takes medication and needs extra rest each day, she faithfully teaches her children and cares for her husband and their home on a daily basis. On her fortieth birthday, I attempted to tease her gently about her age, but she responded cheerfully that she is deeply grateful for every year. It is refreshing to watch someone cherishing the time she spends with her family because she understands the brevity of life.

DEVELOP STRONG RELATIONSHIPS

As you are living life in the midst of homeschooling, it is wonderful to be able to develop strong ties and loving relationships.

Siblings

Even though our two sets of twins are five and a half years apart, we tried to instill in all four of them a deep love for one another and strong bonds. Obviously, a parent cannot demand genuine loving friendships among their children, but there are some things you can do to encourage those special relationships.

First, while our children certainly had playmates, ran around outside with the youngsters from the neighborhood, and developed friendships with the children from church, we did not allow them to have buddies over all the time. We extended hospitality to entire families often, but saved invitations to just one or two friends for special occasions.

Why? It's simple. We valued our children playing together and unexpected young guests often threw unintended wrenches into the mix. Let's say my children are playing well together, but the doorbell rings and one other child is invited in. Instantly, there are conflicts and unexpected issues. Inevitably the atmosphere changes and, perhaps, one or more of my kids wander away from the others. Or, the child who is the age and gender of the guest will leave with their newly arrived friend to play in another room. Either way, the dynamics change.

Yes, I realize that children need to develop conflict resolution skills and, yes, it is necessary for them to learn to get along with others. Yes, it is essential for your children to realize that things do not always go their way. These lessons are important and can and should be taught throughout the years, but these arbitrary visits often trade sibling relationship building for unintended conflict resolution lessons and the timing is not always optimal. You as the parent should, for the most part, decide how often and when other children are invited into your home or back yard.

Occasionally bringing in one or two other children randomly is fine, even good, but for the most part we wanted our children to play with each other. We wanted them to use their imagination to come up with games, develop peacemaking skills with one another, and grow in their sibling relationships. Many, many days were spent with all four of them in their pajamas running around the house simply playing together. I can remember vividly all four of them making blanket forts, putting on plays, playing "office", "poor people", and all the other crazy games they would make up. They were building their relationships with one another in those times of play and, as young adults, they are still friends.

Second, when our children went somewhere together, my husband would encourage it by paying for their activity. Tickets to a movie, ice cream cones, and lunches out together were all put on Dad's tab - with some guidelines, of course. I can still remember the look of shock on my husband's face when the kids went out together with our credit card and charged almost $60 for breakfast. They all got smoothies, the oldest explained.

Thirdly, we encouraged them to share with one another and provided them with one car, which sharpened their peacemaking and negotiating skills. The boys also shared a room which bolstered their friendship. I would often walk down the hall late at night and hear them talking quietly together. Although the girls did not share a bedroom, they did share a bathroom where a lot of the same objectives were accomplished. There they would divide up clothes and make-up and have unfiltered conversations at the lavatory sink.

Encouraging sibling time together and opportunities to share can lead to deep friendships that will be a blessing that lasts for years to come.

Home Schooling Friends

Even as we highly valued our family time and put an emphasis on loving sibling relationships, we came to realize that our entire family benefitted greatly from having strong ties with other homeschooling families and, hopefully, those families benefitted from their friendships with us. Homeschooling is such a unique way of life and (at times) so all-encompassing that the comfort of walking alongside other like-minded families can be very helpful. Having another mom to bounce ideas off, another dad for your husband to ask questions or observe leadership, and children for yours to hang out with on field trips can greatly enrich your lives.

I would encourage you to cultivate those friendships. Invite a homeschooling mom and her children to the park or to see a play, organize a group field trip, or extend an invitation to an entire family for dinner. Walk alongside other similar families and share your unique lifestyle and perspective.

Marriage

> Let marriage be held in honor among all, (Hebrews 13:4a ESV)

You are a homeschooling mother and a homemaker, yes, but you are also a wife. Live life with your husband too. Marriage, like children, needs to be tended and nourished. We were blessed to be near grandparents when our children were young so my husband and I were able to get away for short trips occasionally, but we also hired teenagers as needed for date nights. Outside of your relationship with the Lord, your marriage should be the most important one. While each child should certainly feel loved and cared for, no child should get the impression that he or she is more important to their parent than the other parent.

GETTING IT ALL DONE

Playing vs Schooling

We have several friends with large families whose ages span many years. They divide their children up into groups called "the littles" and "the bigs". Our two sets of twins are almost six years apart and so for many years I, too, was struck by the question, "What to do with 'the littles' while 'the bigs' are doing their school work?"

There always seem to be clashing agendas for these two groups. "The littles" want to play all day while "the bigs" know that they that need to complete their school work. A parent wants both. What to do?

I put together a special box for "the littles" that could only be opened when "the bigs" were working on their lessons. The box contained appealing toys and other items such as magnetic numbers and letters for the refrigerator, coloring sheets and favorite books. "The littles" were excited about their special school box and I changed the items out frequently to keep them interested.

I also scheduled a bath time for "the littles" for the late morning after breakfast and chores. This kept "the littles" occupied for a while so that "the bigs" could work without interruption on their lessons. I would sit on the bathroom floor and monitor "the littles" while they splashed around and played with water toys, foam letters and colorful bath soap and leave the bathroom door open so I could also observe "the bigs" as they did their math and other assignments.

Some families hire a homeschooling teenager or flexible college student to help with "the littles" a couple of mornings a week and some enlist the help of grandparents.

Other families ask their older children to take turns bouncing between school work and playing with "the littles" and some moms just hold the young one her lap while she helps with the school lessons. Some "bigs" don't actually require much assistance. Again, every family is so very different. Remember, depending on the size of your family and the age span of your children, this dilemma usually lasts for just a short season. Soon that young child or children will also be doing school work.

Homemaking

One of the concerns I had about homeschooling was how I would be able to get all of my chores completed while I was teaching and training the children all day. When the children were young, I would clean and straighten things up while they napped and cook while they watched a little video. As a homeschooling mom, I wondered how I would manage everything. I envisioned us sitting at the kitchen table all day with our books and papers spread out everywhere. I imagined myself standing at the white board explaining concepts with a disorganized mess looming behind me. As it turns out, things weren't exactly how I imagined. There were many lessons the "bigs" could work on without direct supervision. And I didn't actually stand at the white board much; in fact, we mostly used it for silly drawings and playing school rather than actual school work. Neither was my house in complete disarray. Here are some ways I managed to squeeze everything in.

Cleaning

When I found out I was pregnant with my second set of twins, I was ordered by my doctor to restrict my activity. We got that news in December, around the same time my husband was discussing what he was going to get me for Christmas with his unmarried friend, Al. Al, even though he did not have wife, brilliantly suggested purchasing maid service for a year. Frankly, it was one of the most generous, thoughtful gifts I have ever received and helped me not only with the cleaning, but with peace of mind.

After that first very difficult year with two small children and two infants, I went back to regularly cleaning our home, but when I started considering homeschooling I asked my husband if we could hire someone to help again and he graciously agreed. This is obviously a luxury that not everyone can afford. For us, it was for just for a short season, but it helped tremendously.

There are other ways to handle the cleaning. First, do a small amount each day. Remember that, during the younger years, children finish their schoolwork early in the day.

Second, allow your children to watch a special show or movie once a week while you do the heavy "don't get in my way" cleaning. One friend told me she devoted one afternoon a week to cleaning while her young children rested in their rooms with books.

Third, relax your standards a little. This will simply have to happen whether you have a maid or are doing it yourself. Your children will be home all day and you will be reading to them, explaining math concepts, and teaching penmanship. I like to have my house tidy, but I came to realize that it is really okay if your home is not perfectly clean and organized all the time. It would almost be weird if it was.

And lastly, know that the season with helpless youngsters who get in the way passes quickly and those same children will soon be your helpers. When my children got old enough to actually help, I discontinued the maid service, typed up a list of cleaning chores with instructions and we all went to work cleaning the house one afternoon a week. And, yes, it was good for them.

Chore Jar

I also kept a chore jar in the kitchen into which I placed small pieces of paper with a variety of cleaning projects specified and explained. This jar came in handy when (for some reason) we had a free afternoon, finished our weekly cleaning early, needed a punishment, or someone made the mistake of complaining that they were bored. The job suggestions in this jar were thought through beforehand and explained on the small pieces of paper that were folded and tucked into the jar. I also made an effort to have all of the needed supplies available. If someone chose a chore that they especially hated they could certainly put it back and trade for another one.

Cooking

As I said earlier, the children worked on their lessons at the kitchen table so I could usually do the preparation for dinner as I oversaw the schoolwork. I depended on my crock pot for the main course quite a bit. Sometimes I would ask one of the girls to bake while I read out loud and at times I would bake or cook as one of the children read out loud.

One winter, when the children were older, the girls spent one evening a week cooking a special dinner. I encouraged Kim, the oldest, to research and choose the menu and, Melanie, the youngest, choose the dessert. The girls usually picked a theme – French, Italian, Greek, or Mexican. They never seemed to choose anything easy to prepare like chicken and green beans; no, they were adventurous and chose challenging dishes such as beef bourguignon and rich chocolate mousse or marinated kabobs with tzatziki sauce and baklava.

After the theme and the menu were decided upon, they would make a grocery list and we would begin our preparation. I would go to the grocery store and Melanie would get busy decorating the dining room complete with mood music. As soon as I got home from the market, Kim would begin the food preparation and Melanie and I would assist.

The boys' jobs included, first, being out of the house as we prepared the meal and, second, arriving at the appointed time ready and excited to eat. The third and most important rule for the boys, of course, was not to criticize or complain if the timing was off, the ingredients were unfamiliar or they should happen not to like the food.

During these evenings we all managed to learn a lot. The girls became more accomplished in planning and preparing an ambitious meal and the boys were further educated in manners and empathy. Hopefully, they also learned valuable lessons about girls that will translate into consideration for their wives. These were challenging evenings, but we did have a lot of fun with this activity.

Laundry

I usually sorted the laundry one specific evening a week and threw a load into the washer right away. Then the first thing the next morning I'd throw the wet clothes in the dryer and begin the process again thereby completing one load before I even finished having my personal devotion. I got a jump start on my day and even saved a little money because energy consumption is less expensive early in the morning or late at night. If possible, I tried to choose a day of the week when we'd (mostly) be home so that I could keep the laundry going all day.

Babysitting Swap

Having rich friendships with other homeschooling families can provide another benefit -- trading babysitting favors. One friend and I regularly traded afternoons where she would either bring her five children to me or I would bring my four to her. The escaping mom would have a few hours to do whatever she needed or wanted to do while the tending mom would watch the children and perhaps got a little housework completed. Meanwhile, the children would have a blast playing together and building great friendships.

Hiring a Weekly Babysitter

Grocery shopping was a challenge for me with four youngsters tagging along and so I asked a trusted neighborhood teen to come over once a week and play with the children while I went to the market. My husband and I determined that getting roped into buying something that was not on my shopping list was about the same price as hiring a babysitter. As any mom knows, children can be particularly persuasive when it comes to expensive boxes of cereal or snacks.

It's Your Time

Because you are not beholden to someone else's schedule, you will not need to take off time for obscure holidays when your husband has to work, parent-teacher conferences, teacher work, or election days. Additionally, we didn't take entire snow days off. When the flurries fell, we would do some school work, go out and play in the snow, come in for hot chocolate, read by the fire, and work on other assignments while our clothes dried. Then we'd go back out to play in the snow.

Even though we did not take all of the days when the public schools closed, paperwork, housework, cooking and planning were always calling my name; so occasionally we would skip a day of school to simply get caught up on life. We did not do this often because I knew that if we did it would only extend the school year into the summer, but sometimes it was especially needed.

I found another way to stretch my time was to meet my obligations less often. What I mean by that is if I got really squeezed for time I could clean the house every other week rather than every week or cook dinner five evenings a week rather than seven and eat leftovers or eggs on an off night. You can use this technique with almost anything where you have control of the schedule.

Sweet Family Time

As you go along on this life journey I encourage you to put a priority on making memories together. Take hikes in the sunshine, eat ice cream on the deck and sit on the porch and talk. Live life together in the midst of homeschooling and always aim to point one another to the Lord Jesus Christ.

Chapter 6

IT'S NOT JUST ABOUT THE BOOKS

> In the same way, let your light shine before others, so that they may see your good works and give glory to your Father who is in heaven.
>
> —Matthew 5:16 ESV

I went through a phase of reading fiction books about Amish people. I loved the stories about the Amish way of life and their unique perspective and I enjoyed curling up in the evenings reading about these fictional characters. My children noticed these books and started teasing me about cultural isolation. They joked that someday I would write for a publication that distributed only to an audience of Amish, homeschooling families who had twins.

Although my children were exaggerating, there can be a temptation to become withdrawn from the world so in this last chapter I would like to encourage you to be an active part of your community. Activities outside of the home and supervised by the parent can enrich a child's learning experience. It can give them practical life skills and allow your family an opportunity to get to know and even be a blessing to those living around you.

Here are some of the ways we became involved in our community.

Hospitality

> Show hospitality to one another without grumbling. (1 Peter 4:9 ESV)

Hospitality is important to us and, I would make the case, important to God. When the children were young, we mostly invited entire families over, but as the children got older we included single people and other friends.

As we prepared to have guests, the work load did fall primarily on me, but I tried to encourage family involvement as much as possible. The girls would usually make a dessert or appetizer and help with the planning and the boys would set up extra chairs and sometimes help set the table or plan a game or activity. Once the guests arrived, I really depended on my husband and children to make our visitors feel welcome while I put the finishing touches on the meal.

When we didn't know our guests well or they didn't know each other, we would sometimes bring out our "question jar" and ask each person around our table to pick and answer a question. The questions randomly ranged from silly ones like "If you were a crayon what color would you be?" to more serious ones like "What are three feelings you've had today". This technique encouraged the quiet person to share and included even the youngest child in the dinner table conversation.

The kids expressed in later years that they grew tremendously during those times of hospitality. Let's face it, sometimes reaching out to others can be a little awkward even for adults, but I believe that there is no better place on earth for a child or teenager to overcome an understandably self-focused tendency than in their own home. We can all learn to get out of our own comfort zone some and hospitality can be a great way to do that.

Volunteering

> For you were called to freedom, brothers. Only do not use your freedom as an opportunity for the flesh, but through love serve one another. For the whole law is fulfilled in one word: 'you shall love your neighbor as yourself.' (Galatians 5:13–14 ESV)

Volunteering is another great way to get out of your comfort zone. Our family served in several ways, including working in the children's ministry in our church, leading worship for our small group Bible studies, ministering at a homeless shelter, setting up and taking down chairs for the church services and special events, and assisting with a neighbor's campaign for local office. Two of our children helped with vacation Bible school for several years, one son coached baseball and soccer for his sibling's teams, and two of our kids provided debate coaching for a local speech club. We even returned to the public school, where our children previously attended, to have our son read to and visit with the kindergarten class on a regular basis. The teacher said that it encouraged her young students to see someone not much older in age reading to the group.

The volunteering exercise that pushed them out of their comfort zone the most, though, was regularly visiting a nursing home and Alzheimer's ward. My children grew by carrying on conversations with folks from another generation with vastly different experiences and perspectives. One of their new friends was over a hundred years old! They would also provide music for the residents, relying on recognizable hymns in hopes that they would trigger memories of God's faithfulness. Sobered by the age and frailty of the residents, our children would set a high priority on sharing the gospel message during these visits.

Mission trips

> (Jesus said) Go therefore and make disciples of all nations, baptizing them in the name of the Father and of the Son and of the Holy Spirit, teaching them to observe all that I have commanded you. And behold, I am with you always, to the end of the age. (Matthew 28:19–20 ESV)

Our kids went on several mission trips through their middle and high school years. One time, they helped deliver toys to underprivileged children in a nearby state, another time they cleaned and painted school buildings in a neighboring county.

They also went on a few trips outside of America. My husband accompanied them three times to an orphanage in Mexico where they painted, built fences, and organized games and activities for the children. As they got older, they traveled to both Poland and Romania where they assisted local churches in their outreach efforts. Our son, Brett, also spent some time in South Korea working at a camp.

Sports

> An athlete is not crowned unless he competes according to the rules. (2 Timothy 2:5 ESV)

We also participated in sports. When our children were really young, they were involved in gymnastics. Later the boys played t-ball and all four of our children played soccer. The boys moved on to baseball, three of the kids played basketball, and one of our sons played football for a season. All four of them were on a swim team for over a decade.

Sports teams for young children are plentiful, but when they reach high school, it can be a little more challenging for those educated at home. This is because many kids play on their school teams. Every state is different, but sometimes homeschooled students are eligible to play on the public school teams. Where we lived during our children's high school years, we had club soccer teams, a homeschool track team, and an available swim team for middle and high schoolers. We took advantage of all three. The swim team, especially, was an excellent experience and an essential part of their high school training as they developed teamwork and leadership skills in addition to gaining physical exercise and expertise.

Fine Arts

> Praise him with tambourine and dance; praise him with strings and pipe! (Psalm 150:4 ESV)

Our children love music and we were blessed to be able to provide them with private lessons for the instruments of their choice. We experimented with some rented instruments before purchasing a flute, guitar, keyboard, and violin. Their instructors encouraged community involvement through festivals, competitions and, of course, recitals. Our kids also played for church worship and our youngest son, James, is minoring in piano at The University of Tennessee.

Melanie, our youngest daughter, would say that one of the most significant components of her high school years was dancing. Registered with a local dance company, she was part of more classes than I can count and participated in more recitals than my poor boys would care to remember sitting through. But she loved it and met many girls from the community. Also in college, she is currently a dance instructor.

All four children participated in many church plays both on and behind the stage. The older twins also took an "Introduction to Theater" class at a local co-op.

Jobs

> Whatever you do, work heartily, as for the Lord and not for men, knowing that from the Lord you will receive the inheritance as your reward. You are serving the Lord Christ. (Colossians 3:23–24 ESV)

Our children also held jobs during their high school years, mostly in the summer. My husband didn't want them beholden to a vacillating schedule that someone else determined each week such as a store or restaurant, so the positions they applied for and accepted allowed family time to remain a high priority. My husband also encouraged the kids to go after jobs that were interesting and beneficial to them. Being swimmers, all four of them worked at the pool where they met some of our neighbors and coached a summer swim team. Our daughters babysat in the neighborhood and our boys dog-sat. Two of our children were piano teachers.

Our oldest son, Brett, was blessed to be hired for an actual internship while still in high school, where he gained practical experience and valuable contacts that he still utilizes today.

Field Trips

> But ask the beasts, and they will teach you; the birds of the heavens, and they will tell you; or the bushes of the earth, and they will teach you; and the fish of the sea will declare to you. Who among all these does not know that the hand of the Lord has done this? In his hand is the life of every living thing and the breath of all mankind. (Job 12:7–10 ESV)

It's a running joke among many homeschooling families that every vacation is a field trip and there is so much truth to that statement. When we went to the beach, we could observe sea creatures, the moon and the tides. As we walked along the sand and swam in the ocean enjoying the fresh air and exercise, we considered the majesty of God in the seemingly endless vast ocean sea. When we went skiing, there were physical skills to master and a glorious terrain to behold. And, Williamsburg, Virginia. Don't even get me started! There is so much history to relive.

We also visited the Creation Museum in Kentucky, toured the Biltmore Estate in North Carolina, hiked many times in the Great Smoky Mountains, visited Washington DC, Chicago, New York City, and explored Yellowstone and Yosemite National Parks. Each new place offered entertainment, family building experiences and educational opportunities. Even visiting Disney World, besides being a lot of fun, taught patience and the "art of standing in line" that some seem to be worried that homeschoolers will miss out on.

There are many other vacations that your family can take that will get you out of your world a little and can make learning come alive for you and your children. They don't have to be lavish or extremely expensive; in fact, because you are not bound by someone else's school schedule often you can explore these places during the off-seasons for significantly discounted prices.

We also took day trips to local places like the zoo, a discovery center, a machine shop, a national laboratory, a mine, a natural bridge, and even Krispy Kreme doughnuts.

Before these trips, I would often require my children to think of a couple of questions to ask the tour guide so that they would gain more from the experience and also learn to be a polite, considerate guest.

Imparting Truth

> Let them give glory to the Lord, and declare his praise in the coastlands. (Isaiah 42:12 ESV)

While homeschooling is not only about the books, it should be about following THE book; the Bible, God's holy and inspired word. Just like the rest of the Christian life, the school in your home should be about glorifying God. The overarching goal of homeschooling is to genuinely offer the very gospel that saved you to your children.

Train your children in the way they should go (Proverbs 22:6), tell them of God's marvelous works (Psalm 96:3), and pray that they walk in the truth (3 John 1:4).

I still pray for my children each morning asking God to protect, care for, and teach them. And I often send out a text or two late in the evening asking "What are you doing" or "How was your day?" A part of me longs for those, albeit exhausting days, when they were all four upstairs tucked sweetly in their beds, but even as I say that, I know that they are in the tender care of the Savior who loves them more than I do.

As I close, let me leave you with the words from a short note that was sent to me along with a delicate small pendant by the founders of Sonlight Curriculum, John and Sarita Holzmann.

> Dear Mom,
>
> On a trip to Israel, John and I learned that Israel allows the sale of its antiquities - something none of the other Mediterranean countries do. And then we were struck by the simple beauty and symbolism of pendants made from the lowly "Widow's Mite" that dates back to the time of Christ.
>
> You may recall the story of Jesus watching people put gifts into the temple treasury. A poor widow came along and put in two small coins - mites.
>
> "I tell you the truth," Jesus said, "this poor widow has put in more than all the others. All these people gave their gifts out of their wealth; but she out of her poverty put in all she had to live on." (Luke 21: 1-4)
>
> I am pleased to give this pendant to you to commemorate the loving sacrifices you make daily to teach your children. I pray it will remind you in years to come that the sacrifices you made to train up your children were, indeed, worth "more than all the others."
>
> Blessings to you,
> Sarita[1]

After laying down your life for many years, giving your efforts to the Lord, and daily crying out for His help, you can confidently send your children out to tackle the good works God has prepared for them (Ephesians 2:10).

> Behold, children are a heritage from the Lord, the fruit of the womb a reward. Like arrows in the hand of a warrior are the children of one's youth. Blessed is the man who fills his quiver with them! He shall not be put to shame when he speaks with his enemies in the gate. (Psalm 127:3-5 ESV)

Bibliography Notes

Introduction

1. Courtney Reissig, *The Accidental Feminist* (Wheaton, Illinois, Crossway, 2015), 152

My Story

1. Paul David Tripp, *Forever* (Zondervan, Grand Rapids, Michigan, 2011), 139-140
2. James Dobson, *Bringing up Boys* (James Dobson Inc., 2001), 85

Chapter One: The Essentials

1. Albert Mohler, Together for the Gospel (2012), Main Session.
2. Greg L. Bahnsen, "Christian Education as Covenant Faithfulness" (Idaho: Covenant Media Foundation, 1993).
3. http://ncfca.org/, accessed January, 2017
4. Melanie Lewis, 2016

Chapter Two: The Home in Home Schooling

1. Tedd Tripp, *Shepherding a Child's Heart*, (Amityville, NY, Shepherd Press, 1995), 233
2. James Dobson, "Childish Irresponsibility" http://www.drjamesdobson.org/Broadcasts/my-family-talk-dr-james-dobson-Broadcast?i=f01f870f-c82c-4228-aba2-b177c1afafba
3. James Dobson, "Common Mistakes – Anger and Verbal Outbursts" http://dobsonlibrary.com/resources/article/15a432f6-29e2-4bdb-a598-4b296b81058a

Chapter Three: The School in Home Schooling

1. http://people.howstuffworks.com/public-schools1.htm
2. http://people.howstuffworks.com/public-schools1.htm
3. Brian Ray, "Research Facts on Homeschooling, March 23, 2016 http://www.nheri.org/research/research-facts-on-homeschooling.html
4. Dave Ramsey, Financial Peace University, Of Mice and Mutual Funds, 2012
5. Brian Ray, "Research Facts on Homeschooling, March 23, 2016 http://www.nheri.org/research/research-facts-on-homeschooling.html

Chapter Four: Choosing Curricula

1. Beverly Hernandez, "Homeschool Co-ops – Benefits of Joint Classes", 2017 http://homeschooling.about.com/od/socialization/p/homeschoolcoop.htm
2. http://en.wikipedia.org/wiki/LibriVox
3. http://en.wikipedia.org/wiki/LibriVox

Chapter Five: Life in the Middle of Your School

1. Dennis Cleveland, Maranatha! Music (1982)

Chapter Six: It's Not Just About the Books

1. Holzmann, Sarita, "The Widow's Mite", https://www.sonlight.com/LP07.html

Printed in the United States
By Bookmasters